Dr. Schulze's
5-Day
LIVER
Detox

Dr. Schulze's
ORIGINAL CLINICAL FORMULAE
Since 1979

Published by
Natural Healing Publications
P.O. Box 9459, Marina del Rey, CA 90292
1-877-TEACH-ME (832-2463)

Library of Congress Catalog
Card Number: Pending
**Create Powerful Health Naturally
with Dr. Schulze's 5-Day LIVER Detox**
ISBN: 0-9761842-4-9

 PRINTED IN THE USA ON 100%
CHLORINE, AND BLEACH-FREE
RECYCLED PAPER, WITH MINIMUM 30%
POST-CONSUMER WASTE (REALLY RECYCLED
WASTE), USING SOY-BASED INKS.

Dr. Schulze's 5-Day LIVER Detox

WARNING

This book is published under the First Amendment of the United States Constitution, which grants the right to discuss openly and freely all matters of public concern and to express viewpoints no matter how controversial or unaccepted they may be. However, medical groups and pharmaceutical companies have finally infiltrated and violated our sacred constitution. Therefore, we are forced to give you the following WARNINGS:

If you are ill or have been diagnosed with any disease, please consult a medical doctor before attempting any natural healing program.

Many foods, herbs or other natural substances can occasionally have dangerous allergic reactions or side effects in some people. People have even died from allergic reactions to peanuts and strawberries.

Any one of the programs in this book could be potentially dangerous, even lethal. Especially, if you are seriously ill.

Therefore, any natural method you learn about in this book may cause harm, instead of the benefit you seek. ASK YOUR DOCTOR FIRST, but remember that the vast majority of doctors have no education in Natural Healing methods and Herbal Medicine. They will probably discourage you from trying any of the programs.

"Feel better, prevent disease and triple your energy with my easy, simple and fast **5-Day LIVER Detox!**"
— *Dr. Richard Schulze*

TABLE OF CONTENTS

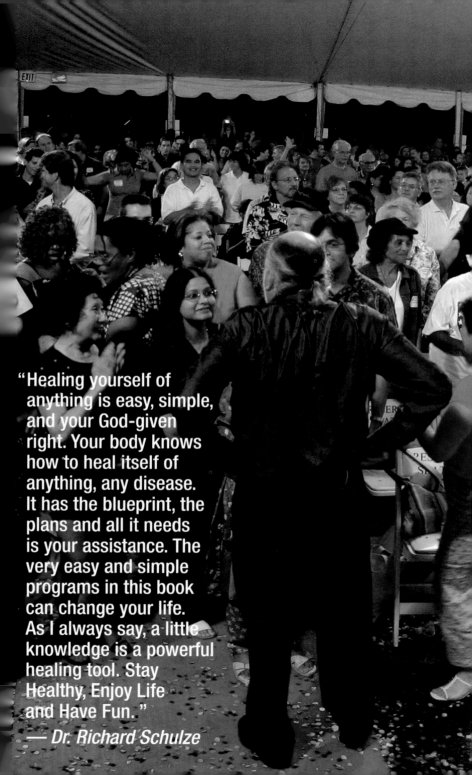

"Healing yourself of anything is easy, simple, and your God-given right. Your body knows how to heal itself of anything, any disease. It has the blueprint, the plans and all it needs is your assistance. The very easy and simple programs in this book can change your life. As I always say, a little knowledge is a powerful healing tool. Stay Healthy, Enjoy Life and Have Fun."
— *Dr. Richard Schulze*

FOREWORD
BY DR. RICHARD SCHULZE

FEEL MORE ALIVE WITH A HEALTHY LIVER

Who knows what some of our ancestors were thinking over a thousand years ago when they came up with the word to describe this organ. I believe they were thinking of the word LIVE, which comes from the word ALIVE, which means to _continue life_. Again, who knows, but they knew one thing for sure… when this organ gets injured, or gets sick, you cannot _continue life_.

Your liver is the LARGEST _solid_ organ in your body. It does more varied and different jobs for you than any other organ. In fact, medical science doesn't know everything it does, and in my opinion never will. What we do know is that it creates glucose, the body's only

chemical that gives us _pure_ energy. It creates digestive fluids needed to digest foods. It creates enzymes that neutralize toxic poisons in your blood. It creates hormones, breaks down fat, kills bacteria and virus, synthesizes protein and stores everything from immune cells to iron to Vitamins A, B-12, D, E, K and on and on and on.

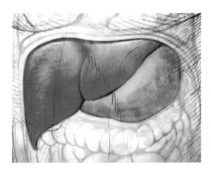

YOUR ULTIMATE ENERGY ORGAN

It's your liver's job to convert carbohydrates you eat into glucose. **Glucose is the primary ENERGY source of the human body.** Your liver makes glucose and then stores it for you as a reserve energy supply. When you need energy anytime 24/7, your liver releases this stored glucose and WOW, you get an energy blast second to none, better than coffee. Keeping your liver healthy and clean simply helps you have all the energy you need, whenever you need it.

YOUR ULTIMATE DETOXIFICATION ORGAN

Your liver is the ultimate detoxification organ in your body. Most of the food you consume is dusted with, dipped in, sprayed, mixed, colored, flavored and preserved with thousands of different toxic chemicals and then packaged in toxic containers. And God only knows what is in the water you drink and the air you breathe?

Everything you eat and drink is digested and travels from your intestines, via your portal vein, to your liver FIRST. Everything that goes into your mouth must first pass through the liver, *and its numerous safety checks*, before entering your bloodstream to feed every cell in your body. One of your liver's most important jobs is to produce enzymes and numerous other chemicals that neutralize and render harmless all the harmful and toxic substances in your food, water and air.

If your liver is clean and healthy, then it also contains millions and millions of immune cells, called macrophages, which literally means *"big eaters"*. These macrophages are the back-up system to your liver's detoxification ability killing and eating bacteria, virus, fungus, parasites and any harmful toxin, poison or chemical that they come in contact with.

CREATE AN ENERGIZED, HEALTHY AND LONG LIFE

Whether you are living the **American Dream**, or the *Japanese, Russian or Chinese*, modern living in most of the civilized world is also a toxic, poisonous and *actually lethal* experience. What is in your food, water and air is trying to create disease and kill you every second of every day. **Thank God for your liver, because it's saving your life, every day**. Think about it, my friends, considering that there are about 100,000 new chemicals floating around in our environment, *and our bodies*, a little flushing, cleaning and protecting of your liver once a year doesn't seem so extreme, does it?

The bottom line, keeping your liver healthy… keeps you healthy, so let's take a look at some of the health benefits of my **5-Day LIVER Detox.**

THE HEALTHY BENEFITS OF DR. SCHULZE'S 5-DAY LIVER DETOX

WHY DO WE NEED TO CLEAN AND FLUSH OUR LIVERS?

As mentioned, it's the liver's job to filter everything we eat and drink and remove anything harmful from our digested food before it enters our bloodstream. It removes cholesterol and harmful fats from eating too much animal food and removes the literally thousands of additives in the food and liquid that we consume.

Your liver removes all of this harmful material from your blood that if left behind, will cause heart attacks, strokes, circulatory disease, cancer, neurological diseases and a hundred other diseases. This is why many doctors will often say that when you have almost any disease, your liver was sick long before your disease developed.

An unhealthy lifestyle and diet causes the liver to be overworked and then congested with this same toxic waste it has removed from your blood. But now, in it's constipated and sick state, your liver can't get the poison out of itself. This accumulated waste eventually causes your liver to get diseased and even causes liver cancer.

Liver flushing and cleansing does just that. It causes the liver to empty its toxic contents, when it is constipated and overloaded with them. Think of it as an enema for the liver.

"Getting well is easy.
All you have to do is…
STOP doing what is
making you sick and
killing you.
START doing what will
heal you and create
powerful health.
Tomorrow is what you
Believe and Do Today."
— *Dr. Richard Schulze*

CHAPTER ONE
WHY CLEANSING YOUR LIVER IS VITAL. YOUR LIVER CLEANS YOUR BLOOD.

Disease doesn't just happen overnight. Heart disease, cancer—most all diseases—develop months, even years after your liver failed to keep your blood clean.

That is its job. 24 hours a day, 7 days a week, 365 days a year, every second of every day, NONSTOP… your liver cleans and detoxifies your blood. Its job is to trap, filter, neutralize, render harmless, kill and eliminate ANYTHING you have inhaled, consumed or absorbed which may be damaging to your body.

Bacteria, fungus, virus, parasites, old pharmaceutical drug residues, alcoholic beverages, old worn out red blood cells, carcinogenic vapors from plastics, toxic household chemicals or just the pesticides, insecticides, preservatives and chemical additives in the food on your dinner plate, natural or man-made toxins, whatever, your liver has to deal with it and it does. There are literally millions of toxic trash bits circulating in your blood and they're hurting every cell in your body.

If your liver didn't continually remove this toxic trash, you would be dead in hours!

Over 72,000 synthetic chemicals have been developed since WWII and less than 2% of them have been tested for toxicity. Many are known to cause birth defects and cancer and to damage the liver, kidneys, and brain. Most have NEVER been tested for long-term effects.

Most people think that even though there are thousands of toxic chemicals found in our air, water, earth and food, that these poisons aren't in our bodies. Most people are wrong.

Analysis of human fat, blood, urine, breath, mother's milk and even semen demonstrate that EVERYONE (especially Americans) carries hundreds of toxic lethal chemicals in their tissues. Dioxins (Agent Orange), PCB's, DDT, Organophosphates, Orangochlorines, the list goes on and on. Most of these toxic chemicals present in our bodies have been linked to the skyrocketing cancer rate and alarmingly high rate of reproductive disease and failure.

Most people also believe that low dose exposure to these chemicals can't possibly harm us, that the government wouldn't possibly allow it. Once again, most people are wrong. Everyone on earth now eats, drinks, and breathes a soup of toxic chemicals that cause health damage at low doses.

If you think you'll get protection by locking yourself up in your house, think again. A recent EPA study concluded that air inside American homes is up to 70 TIMES more polluted than outdoor air and that toxic fumes from common household cleaners cause cancer.

If all this isn't bad enough, toxic radiation from Chinese weapons tests and poisonous industrial chemicals from Japan and Russia arrive in America often within hours of their emissions. Not long ago, deadly bacteria from Africa caused disease outbreaks in Florida. The contamination was found to be caused from the pathogens living in the cracks of African sand particles that were picked up in African desert dust storms, drawn up into the upper atmosphere and then dropped out of the sky with rain in Florida to maim and kill Americans.

The bottom line is, I don't care who you are, and I don't care how healthy you think you might be. I don't care if you live in Tahiti, eat only organic fruit, drink only distilled water, and exercise eight hours a day. If you are a human being who eats, drinks and breathes, and if you live anywhere on this planet, your liver has been attacked, damaged and is possibly even sick.

Your only possible defense is a strong offense, in other words, a strong and healthy liver. And, the best way to maintain a strong and healthy liver is to cleanse it regularly.

PREVENT DISEASE AND PROTECT YOUR LIVER NOW!

The main idea in Natural Healing (as opposed to conventional medicine) is to prevent disease and protect your body, before it gets sick. Your liver (more than any other organ in your body), prevents you from getting sick. Since your liver is the defensive barrier between the things you take into your body and the blood that feeds that body, it is often referred to as your first line of defense. Even conventional doctors will tell you that long before most diseases surface, often the liver was weak and unable to perform its job. That's why it is so important to cleanse your liver on a regular basis.

THE #1 AND #2 CAUSES OF DEATH IN AMERICA ARE DIRECTLY LINKED TO THE LIVER.

Heart attacks and strokes, the #1 cause of death in America, are caused by cholesterol build-up blocking either the coronary or cerebral arteries, which ends up either killing the heart or killing the brain. It's one of the liver's main duties to filter this cholesterol out of your blood.

The #2 cause of death in America is cancer. Everyone now agrees that toxic, carcinogenic chemicals in our environment cause almost all cancers—chemicals that have found their way into the food we eat, the water we drink and the air we breathe. These poisons get into our bloodstream, kill our cells, create tumors, cause cancer, and ultimately kill us. **Another one of the liver's main duties is to eliminate these poisons from our blood.** For either one of these two things to happen, the liver must first fail to do its job.

#1: HEART ATTACKS AND STROKES ARE CAUSED BY HIGH CHOLESTEROL

FACTS

▸ **Over one million Americans will be killed by circulatory disease, heart attacks and stroke, this year alone.**

▸ **Every hour of every day, over 500,000 Americans swallow a pharmaceutical drug to try to lower their cholesterol.**

Your liver has many functions and one of its main ones is balancing the amount of cholesterol in your blood. It is common scientific knowledge and simple Newtonian physics

THIS IS THE DIRECT CAUSE OF 99% OF ALL HEART ATTACKS

and the majority of strokes and other circulatory diseases.

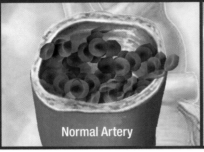

Normal Artery

Clogged Artery

that too much fat in your blood causes your blood to be thicker, which in turn requires your heart to pump harder, which in turn causes hypertension (high blood pressure). When this cholesterol increases and accumulates even more, it can block off critical arteries to your heart and brain, causing heart attacks and stroke. It is your liver's job to filter that cholesterol out, which it does.

But when in turn that cholesterol clogs up your liver, your liver becomes overloaded, and then the excess cholesterol spills off into the bloodstream and ends up clogging your arteries.

The only source of cholesterol that can get into our body is from our food. It doesn't come from our air and it doesn't come from our water—only from our food. And the only food source of cholesterol on the planet is animal food. Being that Americans eat more animal food than almost any other nation on the planet, we as a nation have the highest amount of cholesterol in our bloodstream.

#2: CANCER IS CAUSED BY ENVIRONMENTAL TOXINS AND POISONS

FACTS

▸ **Cancer is the #2 cause of death in America today, killing well over 1/2 million Americans every year!**

▶ **80% of all cancers are a direct result of chemicals in our air, water and food, according to leading experts.**

▶ **More than 72,000 synthetic chemicals are in commercial use today, with approximately 1,000 new chemicals introduced each year.**

▶ **Of those 72,000 plus chemicals, less than 7% have been tested for adverse effects.**

Modern life in America literally surrounds us with poisons and toxic chemicals. They come from our air, water and food, and are absorbed directly through our skin. They are found everywhere, from our household furniture, rugs and construction material off-gassing, to the plastic wrap and containers we store our food and liquids in, to the products we clean our house and body with. THEY'VE GOT US SURROUNDED!

The issue of environmental toxins is complex, and that's because the poisons are coming at us from all directions. They come not only from our food, like cholesterol, but from our water and air, as well. Some of them are actually being assimilated directly through the pores of our skin right at this very moment.

It doesn't take a genius to figure out that we're getting bombarded with more chemicals today than ever before in history. When your liver is weak, these chemical poisons and toxins start to slowly but surely poison every cell in your body, causing numerous diseases that could eventually KILL YOU!

Again, almost all scientists, medical researchers and top cancer specialists now agree… **CANCER is caused by TOXIC and POISONOUS chemicals from our environment that get into our body and irritate, inflame, harm and eventually mutate our bodies' cells.**

In Chapter 1 of this book I expose facts that are almost too horrible to believe, but they speak for themselves. The reality is that in pursuit of the American Dream, we have poisoned our air, water and food. And almost all our modern conveniences are killing us in some way or another. Unless you are ready to drop out to the jungles of Ecuador, there is literally no escaping it. You can live depressed, paranoid or just plain freaked out, or better, you can learn to do something about it.

THE PROBLEM:
DISEASED LIVER

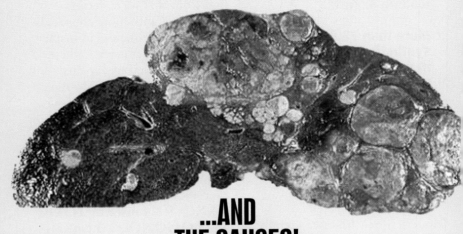

...AND
THE CAUSES!

Junk Food

Poisons And Chemicals

Air Pollution

Water Pollution

CHAPTER TWO
A DAILY DOSE OF POISON: MODERN LIFE IN AMERICA

Your only possible defense is a strong offense. In other words, a CLEAN and STRONG LIVER.

Twenty-four hours a day, 365 days a year, you are bombarded.

THERE IS NO ESCAPE.

RURAL LIVING doesn't stop you from being contaminated by global pollution.

POLITICAL BORDERS won't stop you from being infected with diseases from other parts of the world.

WHAT CAN YOU DO?

Your only possible DEFENSE is a strong OFFENSE, in other words, a clean and strong liver.

I don't care if you live in Tahiti, eat only organic fruit, drink only distilled water and meditate eight hours a day. If you live anywhere on this planet and want to be healthy, and stay that way, you need to flush out your liver and gallbladder... and do it regularly!

Medical doctors often say that before most diseases develop, the liver was malfunctioning and not doing its job. I have heard oncologists (cancer specialists) say that long before a person develops cancer, almost always, the liver was weak and not protecting the patient. This is why the liver is referred to as your first line of defense. Your liver is your defensive barrier between the things you take into your body and your blood. It literally blocks harmful substances from getting into your blood. To explain this let me refer briefly to my book **Create Powerful Health Naturally with Dr. Schulze's 5-Day BOWEL Detox...**

"...The small intestine is where the majority of food absorption takes place; the more surface area to absorb, the better. Each villus (the singular of villi) contains a capillary network which introduces the digested food nutrients into your bloodstream. The portal vein transports this digested food first from your small intestine into your liver and then, if deemed acceptable, onward into your entire circulatory system to feed every cell in your body."

So as you can see, everything you breathe and swallow—food, water, drugs, EVERYTHING— once it is assimilated by your small intestine, everything goes directly to your liver. Even what is in the air you breathe is taken into your bloodstream and then dealt with by your liver. If it is toxic, then your liver creates particular chemicals, like enzymes, that can actually neutralize the poison.

YOU SAY YOU DON'T EAT OR DRINK POISON?

You can't say that anymore. If you live anywhere on this planet, you are breathing, drinking and eating poisons. The FDA says that just the food in the average American grocery cart contains over 50 known poisons and toxic substances. Just read the newspaper or listen to the radio, and you'll hear a current hot news story about a health concern that affects the liver. Most of the stories have to do with our liver cells being hurt, damaged, sometimes even destroyed, by toxic chemicals in our food, air, water and environment and especially by pharmaceutical drugs that have been found, after approval, to be liver killers.

Let me give you just a few examples of extremely common killer poisons that target the liver, that we take into our bodies and blood every day. (I have left out thousands that cause disease and kill other organs; I've just stuck to the liver.)

▸ **1,3-Butadiene, in everything from rugs and rug pads to gasoline, rubber tires, car exhaust and groundwater, is known to cause liver cancer.**

▸ **Benzenes in plastics, polypropylene food and water containers and tobacco cause liver tumors and cancer.**

▶ **Chlorinated water,** whether you drink it or just breathe the vapor from your shower, destroys liver white blood cells.

▶ **Carbon Tetrachloride,** found in groundwater, destroys the liver's enzymes that it creates to render poisons harmless.

▶ **DEHP (Diethylhexyl- phythalate)** that is in many plastics, food wraps and even used to make blood storage bags (and can leach into the stored blood) is a killer to the liver.

▶ **Dioxins,** which are common in pesticides, herbicides and now found worldwide in air, water, animal products and even in human livers, kill the liver, too.

▶ **Ethanol,** in all alcoholic beverages, causes cirrhosis of the liver and kills liver cells.

▶ **Ethylene Oxide,** an anti- bacterial that is gassed onto almost all herbs sold in America today. Even 95% of organically grown herbs after harvesting are gassed with this toxic chemical. Dr. Schulze's

American Botanical Pharmacy is one of the only companies in the world that doesn't use chemically gassed herbs that cause liver damage, promote cancer and mutate unborn children.

▶ **Glycol Ethers,** in anti- freeze, glue, paint, sealants, chalking compounds, circuit boards and ink, kill liver cells.

▶ **Nitrosamines,** in baby nipples and pacifiers, soaps, cosmetics, food additives, food containers, pesticides, insecticides and herbicides, cause liver cancer.

▶ **Styrene,** a very common plastic used in food containers, water bottles, carpets and paper, destroys liver enzymes that protect you.

▶ **Trichloroethylene,** found in dry cleaning fluid, paint, glue, cleaners, degreasers, insecticides, drain cleaners and ink, kills liver cells.

My personal toxic horror pick is PCBs (Polychlorinated Biphenysis) from transformer leakage, and used in copy papers, paints, plastics, flame retardants, glues, adhesives, coolants, inks, common furniture fabric protectors and is now found in groundwater WORLDWIDE. This common, but powerfully toxic and poisonous chemical, kills liver cells and causes cancer and fetal death. This is a big one. You definitely have PCBs in your house in everything from your shower curtains to your bed mattresses to your children. You heard me right. **This chemical is commonly found in the blood and tissue of newborn babies.**

And finally, the **Vinyl Chloride** scandal. A few years back, it was all over every news channel that the chemical industry in America has been accused of not disclosing how toxic many common household chemicals and ingredients are. They were further accused of discussing this in closed-door corporate meetings, and subsequently covering up how poisonous and toxic some commonly used chemicals are. Way back in the 1950s and 1960s workers at the chemical plants that produced **Vinyl Chloride**, a very common plastic used in everything from plastic food wraps to PVC **(PolyVinyl Chloride)** water pipes, were found to have the bones inside their fingers partially dissolved, along with skin damage, nerve damage and

immune cell destruction, leading to cancers of the brain, lung, kidney and, you guessed it, the liver.

THE SHOCKING TRUTH

You've heard it before, the AIR you breathe (we inhale 15,000 quarts of air every day), the WATER and LIQUID you drink and the FOOD you eat is loaded with toxic poisons. Your entire living environment is a chemical swimming pool.

FACTS

▸ **Over 72,000 new synthetic chemicals have been developed since WWII and less than 2%**

of them have been tested for toxicity. Many are known to cause birth defects, cancer and damage the liver, kidneys and brain.

▶ Most have NEVER been tested for long-term effects.

▶ Many people think that even though there are thousands of toxic chemicals found in our air, water, earth and even in our food, that these poisons aren't in our bodies.

▶ Analysis of human fat, blood, urine, breath, mother's milk and even semen demonstrate that EVERYONE on this planet (not just those that live near big cities and pollution sources), but EVERYONE (especially Americans) carry hundreds of toxic lethal chemicals in their tissues—Dioxins (Agent Orange), PCB's, DDT, Organophosphates, Organochlorines...the list is very long. Most of these toxic chemicals present in our bodies have been linked to the skyrocketing cancer rate and alarming high rate of reproductive disease and failure.

OK, so these poisonous chemicals are in our bodies, but can this low dose exposure really hurt us? The government wouldn't allow it—people are just being paranoid.

▶ Joe Thornton, a biologist at Columbia University's Center for Environmental Research, says that everyone on earth now eats, drinks and breathes a soup of toxic chemicals that cause health damage at low doses, and that these toxic chemicals have already begun to cause large scale damage to the public health, including increasing cancer rates and impaired child development.

▶ Thornton and his wife Margie are expecting their first child. Thornton said, "My wife (being an Average American) has accumulated hundreds of industrial compounds in her tissues, and these substances have already crossed the placenta and entered the baby's bloodstream. My semen (being an Average American) contains scores of pollutants that may have damaged the DNA that I contributed to the baby." Thornton continued, "My baby is awash in industrial chemicals."

▸ **Even the Food and Drug Administration has warned that there are over 50 different known poisons and toxic substances just in the Average American's grocery cart. These chemicals combined cause hundreds of different diseases and eventually kill you.**

Maybe each separate low chemical dose isn't enough to kill you, but every day you are exposed to a concentrated cocktail of literally thousands of lethal toxic chemicals—even in your food. Some people say that food and household products couldn't contain dangerous chemicals, again, that the government wouldn't allow it.

THE AVERAGE AMERICAN'S HOME IS REALLY A TOXIC GAS CHAMBER.

Tens of thousands of different chemicals have been used to create the modern American **"way of life."** Cancer-causing vapors off-gas from most common household carpets, because they are made from petrol-chemicals and cause liver and kidney damage. Don't worry about your poisonous insecticides and oven cleaners that you keep under the sink or in your garage, what's in your drapes, wood furniture, plastics, beds, and even your clothing is poisoning you faster. To make matters worse, American homes and workplaces are now so energy efficient (air tight) that toxic chemicals build up to lethal concentrations.

FACTS

▸ **The average American home has more toxic chemicals than a chemistry lab did less than 100 years ago.**

▸ **Americans on average spend 90% of their life living indoors.**

▸ **A recent EPA study concluded that air inside American homes is up to 70 TIMES more polluted than outdoor air and that toxic fumes from common household cleaners cause cancer.**

- **The National Institute of Occupational Safety and Health has found over 2,500 toxic chemicals just in common cosmetics that cause cancer tumors, reproductive disease and mutate unborn children.**

- **According to a study by the American Chemical Society, taking a shower leads to a greater exposure to toxic chemicals than if you drink the water, because the chemicals evaporate out of the water and are inhaled. In fact, in the average 10 minute shower, the human body absorbs as much chlorine as if you drank 20 gallons of tap water.**

All organophosphate insecticides and pesticides like DDT and hundreds of others that are still used, were derived from Adolph Hitler's Nerve Gas that he developed and used to kill millions of Jews. We stole his formula after WWII and "adapted it" and now it is coming back to haunt us.

If all of this isn't bad enough, toxic radiation from Chinese weapons tests and poisonous industrial chemicals from Japan and Russia arrive in America often within hours of their emissions. In 2001, deadly bacteria from Africa caused disease outbreaks in Florida. The contamination was found to be caused from the pathogens living in the cracks of African sand particles that were picked up in African desert dust storms,

As many as 50 million Americans have been poisoned by radioactivity in their tap water.

Toxins such as carbon monoxide, lead, insecticides and pesticides fill the air you are breathing right now.

drawn up into the upper atmosphere and then dropped out of the sky with rain in Florida, to maim and kill Americans.

The American chemical industries, power companies, petrol-chemicals, plastics, manufacturing, mining, farming, might be getting a bit cleaner every year, BUT, even if we stop making and using ALL chemicals right now . . . many experts report that just our past chemical mistakes will still linger and continue to haunt us, create disease, cause cancer and **EVEN KILL OUR GRANDCHILDREN'S GRANDCHILDREN.**

POISON MEDICINE

Hippocrates, the so-called father of modern medicine (he was actually an herbalist) said, "Physician, do no harm" when he stated his basic philosophy of treating patients. He would be spinning in his grave on this one. Recently, the FDA banned numerous common

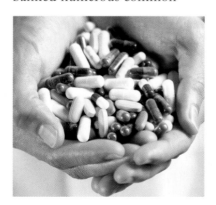

pharmaceutical drugs *suspected* of hurting and KILLING people, killing thousands of people for that matter. **Most people reading this book probably had a relative use one or more of these drugs— maybe you even used them yourself.** One of the drugs was **Propulsid**, the nighttime heartburn drug, that despite the 1993 warning that it caused heart rhythm disorders was kept on the market. It is *suspected* of killing hundreds of people. Also, despite that it was *suspected* to have killed eight children in pre-clinical trials, no one told this to pediatricians who widely prescribed it to infants for common digestive disorders. "We never knew that," said Jeffrey A. Englebrick, a heavy equipment welder in Shawnee, Kansas, whose three-month old baby boy, Scott, died after taking Propulsid. "To me, they used my baby as a guinea pig to see if this drug would work." By the time this drug was pulled off the market, it was *suspected* of killing many children, but the manufacturer had already made 2.5 billion dollars on its sales. Other drugs that were recently banned (that you may still have in your medicine cabinet) and are *suspected* of maiming and killing are:

▶ **Redux, a diet pill, *suspected* in hundreds of deaths.**

▶ **Raxar, an antibiotic that is *suspected* of killing by disrupting heart rhythm.**

▶ **Posicor, a blood pressure medication, again *suspected* in hundreds of deaths due to heart rhythm disruption.**

▶ **Lotronex, a drug for treating irritable bowel, *suspected* of killing many and requiring many users to have their colons removed.**

Of course, many banned drugs are *suspected* of killing the patient by destroying their liver, such as Duract, a painkiller, suspected of causing liver failure and other deaths but...

The winner is... Rezulin. This drug was taken off the market and is *suspected* of being one of the biggest drug scandals in years. This diabetes drug was approved in 1997 and is *suspected* of numerous liver failures and hundreds and hundreds of deaths. Scandal has rocked both the drug manufacturer and the FDA on this one. Apparently pressure, corruption and subsequent cover-up is *suspected* in the drug's approval. And, it is *alleged* that people's jobs were threatened at the FDA, if they didn't cooperate. The drug made over 2 billion dollars in the few short years, before it was recently banned. The medical doctor in charge of this drug company told the FDA that liver damage from this drug was the same as in the placebo group, but in fact it was almost 400% greater. Currently, it is unknown how many people got liver damage or died from using this drug.

FACTS

▶ **The National Cancer Association concluded a 15-year study proving that women who work at home are over 50% more likely to get cancer.**

▶ **Breast cancer rates have skyrocketed in the last 20 years; IT IS THE #1 KILLER OF WOMEN. Even common bleach has been linked to causing breast cancer, along with laundry detergents, household cleaners and pesticides.**

Bleach has also been linked to reproductive failure in men and behavioral problems in children.

Even when we try to do some good and protect people (and even children) by putting flame retardants in all foam furniture and television and computer chassis, we don't really protect them. Well, the most common one, EBDE, is now found in women's breast tissue and breast milk and the potential nightmare is so big that most countries in the world have now banned its use, but American homes and offices are swimming in it.

▶ **Actor Michael J. Fox has Parkinson's Disease. It has now been discovered that numerous other people that worked on the same television and movie sets with him over two decades ago also have Parkinson's Disease, far too many people to be a coincidence. Medical authorities now call this type of incidence a "cluster" outbreak. And even though this and many other diseases are not considered contagious, facts prove that they do "attack" in "clusters" and are now being linked to toxic chemical exposure. Many nervous system**

diseases are now being linked to insecticides and pesticides.

▶ **Allergies, Fibromyalgia, Chronic Fatigue Syndrome, arthritis, diabetes, asthma, immune system suppression, Lupus, Multiple Sclerosis, heart and circulatory disease, Alzheimer's, Parkinson's, Lou Gehrig's and almost all other degenerative nerve disorders, depression, schizophrenia, liver disease, kidney disease, infertility, impotency, reproductive disease, hormonal imbalance, can all be induced by toxic chemical exposure.**

ARE OVER-THE-COUNTER DRUGS SAFE?

First, many of the common drugs now sold over the counter, without prescriptions, were prescription drugs only a few years ago. Over-the-counter drugs are very potent and are also suspected in killing their users. Just simple aspirin and aspirin substitutes like Acetaminophen,

(the active ingredient in Tylenol, Excedrin and an ingredient in Percocet, Vicodin, Sinutab, Sudafed and many more drugs) have been exposed as harmful to your liver, even killing you if you overdose. Medical doctors and government officials said they were basically shocked at this information, but I really don't know exactly why, since it has been published for years. Although the deaths are due to overdose, painkillers are the most common drugs that people take more than the recommended dosage of, ignoring the instructions and just literally sucking a bunch of pills right out of the bottle.

OK, so now I think it's safe to say that if you are a human, living anywhere on this planet, breathing, eating and drinking, that your Liver has been attacked, damaged and is maybe even sick. So, what the heck do we do NOW?

YOUR LIVER AND GALLBLADDER

Knowing how to clean and protect them can SAVE YOUR LIFE

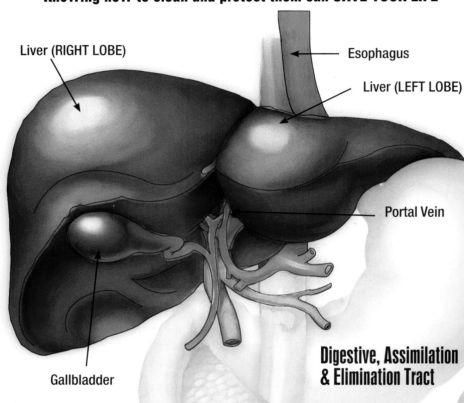

Liver (RIGHT LOBE)

Esophagus

Liver (LEFT LOBE)

Portal Vein

Gallbladder

Digestive, Assimilation & Elimination Tract

Liver cleansing and detoxification is one of the most important things you can do for your health.

CHAPTER THREE
ANATOMY AND PHYSIOLOGY OF THE LIVER AND GALLBLADDER

Your Liver is your Life Force, the source for your ENERGY.

This chapter is for anyone who wants to know more about their liver and gallbladder, where they are, what they do and how and why they get sick.

You do not need to know this information in order to flush out your liver and gallbladder. If you are not one for anatomy and physiology, NO PROBLEM. Just skip to Chapter 5 and I'll tell you how to do my 5-Day LIVER Detox.

THE LIVER

Although your medical doctor would like you to believe that they have figured your liver out and got it all down, the reality is that your liver is the most metabolically complex organ in the entire human body, more than even your brain. It has numerous different microscopic functional units and is as complex and infinite as outer space. One of the main reasons I know God was a Natural Healer (and NOT a medical doctor) is the liver itself. It is so incredibly complex that you know it's best to just leave it alone and create a healing lifestyle for it, and DON'T TOUCH IT, HANDS OFF. Now, let me try to boil it down and make understanding the functions of the liver as simple as possible.

Your liver is the largest organ inside your body. It weighs around three pounds. It is on your right side under your lower ribs. The underneath of your liver is concave, because it covers your stomach, duodenum, hepatic flexure of the colon, right kidney and right adrenal. Blood passes through your liver, especially blood from your digestive organs, which contain end-products of digestion and nutrition, before this blood enters your general circulation to the rest of your body. If I were to divide the two main tasks of your liver, they would be ENERGY/NUTRITION and DETOXIFICATION.

ENERGY AND NUTRITION:

Your liver is your Life Force, the source for your ENERGY.

Your liver synthesizes the sugar glucose from carbohydrates or starches that you eat. Glucose is the most important carbohydrate in your body's metabolism. It could just be called PURE ENERGY, because it is used by your brain and every other cell of the body for just that: ENERGY. Excess

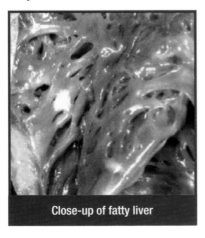
Close-up of fatty liver

glucose is stored in your liver as glycogen and is ready to be converted back to glucose, if any energy is needed. Your liver also stores other SUPER ENERGY NUTRIENTS like Vitamin B-12 and Iron to be used any time you need a turbo-charge.

Your liver also makes vitamins, clotting factors and amino acids. It makes cholesterol that you need to produce steroid hormones (sex hormones) and other important metabolic chemicals. It also makes the lipoproteins (like HDL's) that transport fat around in your blood. (Too much cholesterol in your blood, causing coronary arterial blockages, is from eating too much animal food and rarely from a liver gone haywire.) The liver stores other vitamins too, like A, D, E and K.

DETOXIFICATION:

Your Liver is the Blood Detoxification organ in your body.

The liver recycles and removes worn out blood cells. Each red blood cell has a life span of 120 days (4 months). Once it is old and its time is up, macrophages, big eating white blood cells in your liver, eat the red blood cell. Every

RBC (red blood cell) contains hemoglobin. Hemoglobin is the iron-containing pigment in your blood that makes it red, which carries the oxygen from your lungs to all the cells of your body. Your liver recycles this iron, stores it for later use or turns it into bile, which it excretes as a digestive juice.

Bile stimulates digestion, emulsifies fats, stimulates peristalsis (the muscular waves of the intestines), and is a natural laxative and a natural digestive antiseptic.

Bile contains bilirubin, a yellow-orange pigment from the iron in the hemoglobin from the dead red blood cells that macrophages ate. Phew… if you didn't catch that one, don't worry. Remember, getting well is easy.

Now for you numbers freaks, each red blood cell has over 200 million hemoglobin molecules in it and you have over 35 trillion red blood cells, so that's over 7,000,000,000,000,000 (how the heck do you say this number) hemoglobin molecules that your liver has to recycle, or over 58,000,000,000,000 (58 trillion) hemoglobin molecules every day.

OK, let's get simple. The liver detoxifies, metabolizes, renders harmless and eliminates harmful toxic poisons, chemicals and substances from your blood. It produces many different enzymes that actually convert toxic poisons into harmless chemicals and then they are eliminated in the bile that your liver excretes.

A small list of the substances that your liver detoxifies and renders harmless are alcoholic drinks, street drugs, pharmaceutical drugs, insecticides, pesticides, food additives, environmental toxic chemicals, parasites, bacteria and viruses. So, one of the liver's main jobs is to eliminate toxins, chemicals, poisons and drugs from your body. Then, it only makes sense that the more intake you have of toxic substances, the harder it is on your liver, the more work it has to do. This makes a great case for organic food. It not only tastes better and is more nutritious, but it doesn't overwork or deplete your liver.

The liver also has to metabolize and render harmless anything that causes increased ammonia in the body. The main culprit here is animal food. When animal food is digested it forms ammonia (an alkaline gas), which is absorbed by your intestines into your blood to be hopefully converted into urea by your liver to be removed by your kidneys. Americans, (being the highest consumers of animal food on the planet per person), have a constant overproduction of ammonia gas in the intestines, which in turn weakens the liver and promotes hepatic coma or paralysis of the liver. Substances that contain ammonia (besides animal flesh, organs, eggs and milk), are mainly drugs, such as sedatives, tranquilizers, anesthetics, analgesics (pain relievers) and diuretics.

AT HOME EXPERIMENT: Take two aspirin and place them in a spoon, hold the spoon over a candle (or the stove), until the aspirin melt. WOW! Ammonia city.

For years in my clinic, I saw patient after patient with liver trauma and even acute failure that caused hepatic comas worse than alcohol, drugs and toxic poisons. It was caused by fad high protein diets. These diets have come and gone and the

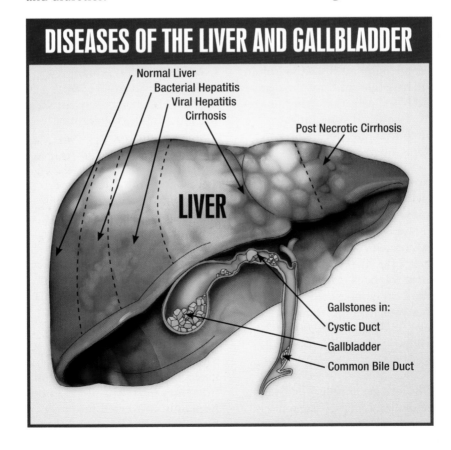

DISEASES OF THE LIVER AND GALLBLADDER

Normal Liver
Bacterial Hepatitis
Viral Hepatitis
Cirrhosis

Post Necrotic Cirrhosis

LIVER

Gallstones in:
Cystic Duct
Gallbladder
Common Bile Duct

current ones are The Zone and Atkins. These diets (like any diet) can cause weight loss, but they can also skyrocket your ammonia levels and paralyze your liver. This is a double whammy, because your liver now cannot process all of this added cholesterol that you are eating more and more of. And, this alone could give you a heart attack or stroke. Granted, you will look fit and trim in the hospital bed or the casket, but better to have a healthy liver, than to be sick or dead.

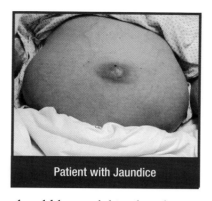

Patient with Jaundice

JAUNDICE: WHEN YOUR LIVER GETS SICK.

As I have discussed, one of the liver's primary jobs is the production of bile, which is its waste product and also a great digestive system aid, among many other things. When the liver gets sick, it gets constipated, and the bile, instead of getting released, backs up in the body. Remember the part before about the 58 trillion hemoglobin molecules that the liver has to process EVERY DAY from the dead red blood cells? Well, when the liver backs up with bile (which contains bilirubin, an orange-red iron pigment from the old hemoglobin that the liver eats) and at the same time the liver can't continue to clean all the 58 trillion a day recently dead orange-red hemoglobin molecules out of your blood—well, in a very short time you have all this excess circulating orange-red bilirubin and hemoglobin. And what color do you think you are going to turn? You guessed it, ORANGE-RED. When your sclera (the whites of your eyes), your skin and even your urine takes on a orange-red color, this is called Jaundice and is a good sign that your liver is very constipated. It is that simple. This is why one of the major cleansing and detoxifying aids that I used in my clinic was a liver/gallbladder flush, to unconstipate the liver and get the bile flowing again. There are 2 main types of Jaundice and they are referred to as Intra Hepatic (inside your liver) and Extra Hepatic (outside of your liver), referring to where it is thought the trouble is.

DISEASES OF THE LIVER

NORMAL LIVER

RECENT HEPATIC INFARCTION
Liver death due to either a blockage or loss of oxygen-rich blood flow to the liver.

STEATOSIS (FATTY LIVER)
This condition often occurs when there is too much fat in the diet.

METASTATIC ADENOCARCINOMA
Cancer that originated in another organ (such as the pancreas, thyroid or kidneys) and then quickly spread to the liver.

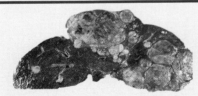

HEPATOCELLULAR CARCINOMA
Cancer originating in the liver. Usually due to a previous liver ailment such as Cirrhosis, Hepatitis or even fatty liver.

HEMOSIDEROSIS
Due to iron overload of the liver, most often from blood transfusions, pharmaceutical drugs or even iron poisoning.

INTRA HEPATIC JAUNDICE

The most common causes of Hepatitis (which just means liver inflammation) and Intra Hepatic Jaundice are drugs, alcohol, liver damage, almost any virus, bacteria, fungus, fad heavy animal protein weight loss diets and viral hepatitis.

VIRAL HEPATITIS

There are currently six known types of Viral Hepatitis. The most commonly known are Hepatitis A, Hepatitis B and what used to be referred to as Hepatitis non-A, non-B which is now called Hepatitis C, and Hepatitis D, E and G. Soon, we will discover so many more that we will run out of letters of the alphabet and have to start giving them names like tropical storms and hurricanes, like Hepatitis Harry. Currently there is a medical mass panic to vaccinate for Hepatitis C. This dangerous vaccination is even given to children born in hospitals in NYC within hours after birth and most school kids in California. But, the only real prevention is to STOP doing what hurts your liver (like drugs and toxins), and START living a healthy liver lifestyle. As I said earlier, the liver's job is to neutralize poisons and toxins and the more a person or child

is bombarded with poisons, the weaker the liver becomes. What poisons, you ask? Well, when was the last time you were around a typical American kid and watched him eat, or any adult for that matter? Weak livers have less resistance to infections. We will never get rid of germs and viruses. As I always say, the only defense is a strong offense, which means building a strong healthy body. The massive amount of hepatitis infections all around America is just a reflection that we have beaten up our livers for too long.

EXTRA HEPATIC JAUNDICE

The most common cause of Extra Hepatic Jaundice is some type of blockage. Sounds like my theory of all diseases being caused by blockage,

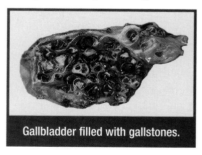
Gallbladder filled with gallstones.

doesn't it? And the major blockage is gallstones stuck in the gallbladder and bile ducts. Over a half million people this year in America will have their gallbladders carved out of them by medical doctors. Medical doctors are so absolutely stupid. FLUSH IT OUT, don't CUT IT OUT.

Minor Jaundice or liver constipation can go on for years almost unnoticed, causing all sorts of health-related problems. Neurological diseases, neuromuscular diseases, paralysis, chronic fatigue, immune system depression and disorders, cancers, heart disease, stroke, hypertension, high cholesterol, every digestive disorder from indigestion to constipation, diabetes, dementia, depression, painful and stiff joints, sexual dysfunction, eyesight problems... the list is almost endlesssssssssss.

Many old sage doctors used to say when you have someone that has cancer, you have a patient who had a sick liver three to five years ago. I will go a step further, with any sick patient and with any disease we need to look at the liver and get it clean. This is why in my clinic, EVERYONE, EVERY SINGLE PATIENT, had to do my **5-Day LIVER Detox** along with my Liver/Gallbladder Flush. The bottom line:

"Let the liver get run down and congested and you will become toxic and weak. Keep the liver healthy and you will be protected from chemical poisons, disease, feel great and have TONS of energy."

HEPATITIS-C AND OTHER VIRAL AILMENTS

Here are some names you may have heard of who are among the 4.5 MILLION Americans living with Hepatitis C: Pamela Anderson, David Crosby, Naomi Judd, Larry Hagman, Jack Kevorkian, Natalie Cole, Natasha Lyonne, Dusty Hill (ZZ TOP), Steven Tyler...the list goes on and on. You could assume, since most of these people are musicians and actors, they simply contracted the disease through hard partying, but you'd be wrong. The fact is most of them contracted Hepatitis C from blood transfusions.

Hepatitis C often leads to chronic liver infections, cirrhosis of the liver (scarring, deformity and non-functioning liver cells), hepatocellular necrosis (liver cell death) and eventually hepatocellular carcinoma (liver cancer) and liver failure and transplantation. It is the beginning of the end for many.

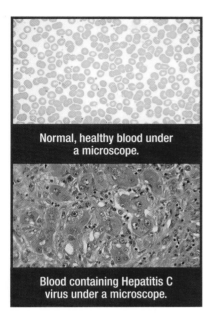

Normal, healthy blood under a microscope.

Blood containing Hepatitis C virus under a microscope.

Author Ken Kesey, poet Allen Ginsberg, blues legend Willie Dixon and baseball's Mickey Mantle all died from liver disease soon after contracting Hepatitis C.

If you, or anyone you know, has Hepatitis C, you were probably informed by your doctor that cancer, cirrhosis and ultimately a liver transplant would be your future. If you are the Average American, your doctor would be right. However, if you decide not to be the Average American, and make positive, healthy changes in your lifestyle, well, you can expect a long, healthy life regardless of any virus that may be lurking in your body, including Hepatitis C.

So instead of waiting for the virus to kill your liver, I've got a better idea...

First, I am a Natural Doctor who knows your body can heal itself of anything, any disease. But medical doctors say that most diseases are incurable and that there is nothing you can do. I suggest my approach.

In the past, it was believed that once you were infected with Hepatitis C, that there was nothing you could do and your body had no defense. However, current medical research has focused on virus specific immune T cells in your body that go to your liver and destroy the HCV (Hepatitis C Virus).

New research released just last year showed two types of specific T cells (T-4 and T-8) can kill the virus. From this research I quote: *"Several groups have reported an excellent correlation between a robust and persistent T cell response and viral clearance during Acute-C viral infections. Evidence also suggests that this immune response is maintained for several years following recovery from the infection. Therefore, Persistent-C virus infection is now associated with a poor T cell response."*

OK, so now the question is how do you get, build and create, a "robust" and "persistent" T cell response?

Let me make another point here. According to most oncologists, everybody has cancer, meaning that everybody has cells in their body that become malignant cells, every day. **Most of us also have strong enough immune cells and immune chemicals that destroy these cancer cells every day, too. That is why most of us do not have cancer.**

I used to always say to my cancer patients that I am not so worried that you have cancer, but what I am very concerned about is *why isn't your immune system killing and eating up the cancer cells in your body?* Why is your immune system NOT taking care of business? Why is your immune system NOT working? With cancer, AIDS, Hepatitis or any virus, or any disease for that matter, the real question is why isn't your body doing its job and protecting you? In Immunology 101 on the first day of class, you learn that your immune system's main job is to kill the bad guys, the harmful bacteria, virus, fungus, disease, whatever, and keep you healthy and alive. This is the primary job of your immune system!

Over the next few decades, many Americans will find themselves hosts to a wide variety of virus from herpes, to hepatitis to HIV—there is no escaping it. But, being a host to a virus and actually getting sick from the virus are two very different things. **What makes the difference between carrying the disease and actually getting the disease is the health of your immune system.** I always say the only defense is a powerful offense, which is building and maintaining a powerful immune system.

OK, so again, the question is how do you get, build and create, a "robust" and "persistent" T cell response?

DR. SCHULZE'S HEALING PROGRAM FOR HEPATITIS

1 Get more nutrition into your body! You can't build powerful immune cells and a powerful immune system on junk food, pizza and beer.

My suggestion is to flood your blood with massive amounts of vitamins, minerals and other

nutritional building blocks that your body needs to build T cells and a "robust" immune system. And, the best way I know how to do this is by taking **SuperFood Plus** two times daily. **SuperFood Plus** is organic and clean, so it doesn't hurt your liver and pollute your body, like many nutritional products. It is also so easy to assimilate into your blood, so it won't tap your energy—it will give you energy.

2 Powerful, high-quality and concentrated Echinacea extracts have been proven to measurably increase the number of T cells in your body. (Here is the

"ROBUST" the doctors were talking about.) Echinacea has also been proven to stimulate these T cells into a higher level of activity (here is the "PERSISTENT" the doctors were talking about) and cause a significant decrease in reoccurring viral infections. Echinacea is a *specific* for Hepatitis C. I suggest taking one bottle of Echinacea Plus, the first week of every month, for the rest of your life!

3 The phytochemicals in my **L-GB Formula** are proven to bind to, coat and protect your liver cells from damage from attacking micro-organisms, including viruses. I would do my

5-Day LIVER Detox immediately and in addition, make my **L-GB Formula** something that you never leave home without. Take it at least every other week, 2 droppersful three times a day.

My friends, I have always said you can heal yourself of

anything, just STOP doing what is making you sick and START doing what will create powerful health. Amen!

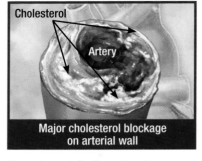

Major cholesterol blockage on arterial wall

THE GALLBLADDER

The gallbladder is a pear-shaped sac on the underside of the right lobe of the liver that stores bile from the liver. While in the gallbladder, the bile is concentrated by removing water. The bile is released through the cystic duct, which joins the hepatic duct from the liver to create the common bile duct, which empties into the duodenum (the beginning of the small intestine).

Bile is not only the waste product of the liver that carries away the neutralized poisons, but, as stated previously, also stimulates digestion, aids digestion by emulsifying fats, stimulates peristalsis (the muscular waves of the intestines), is a natural laxative and a natural digestive antiseptic.

When the bile contains too much cholesterol from eating too much animal food (or for some people ANY animal food), the cholesterol can't be kept in solution anymore and forms very hard stones and rocks. These can form in the gallbladder and also the bile ducts, causing Extra Hepatic Jaundice.

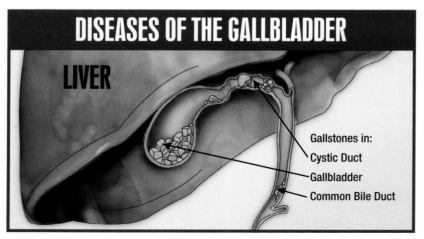

DISEASES OF THE GALLBLADDER

LIVER

Gallstones in:
Cystic Duct
Gallbladder
Common Bile Duct

Get more nutrition into your body! You can't build powerful immune cells and a powerful immune system on junk food, pizza and beer.

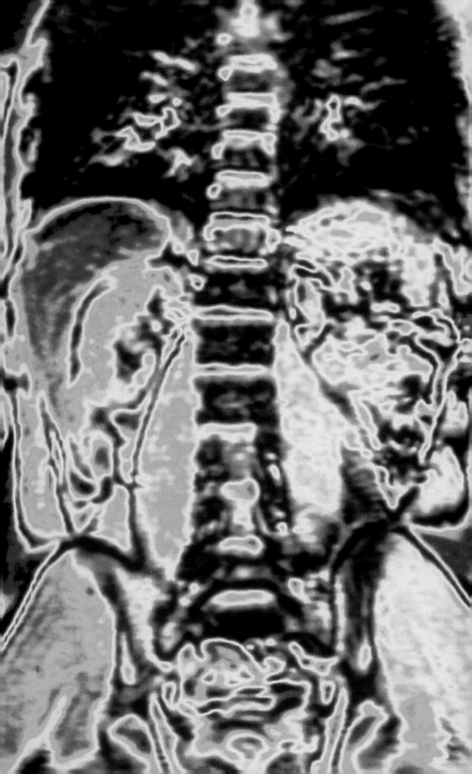

CHAPTER FOUR
A LOOK INSIDE YOUR BODY

How can you continue to live in America and keep your liver clean and healthy?

Teaching in many universities for over 20 years, I had the wonderful opportunity to dissect and examine numerous cadavers to show students what the liver and gallbladder actually looks like, which, believe me, is usually very different from the picture perfect anatomy books.

Often in bodies of people over 60, the internal organs are in such a mess that it is very difficult for students to identify things. They smell so bad that students would run from the room and vomit. One time, I had a student actually vomit in the cadaver, which in turn caused almost every student in the class to involuntarily start vomiting all over the laboratory. After that incident, I almost always tried to get the bodies of younger people killed prematurely due to an accident (rather than disease), so the internal organs would be more normal and less diseased.

What was surprising to me at first was how many young, supposedly healthy individuals would have fairly normal looking internal organs, but when you got to the liver and gallbladder, well, it was like an alien encounter.

Often the liver was shaped drastically different, swollen much larger than normal, filled with bloody fluids, pus, tumors, scar tissue and parasites. Sometimes there was so much swelling that the liver had doubled in size and extended way beyond its normal area, even into the area normally occupied by the spleen and colon.

The gallbladder was often really frightening to students, again being stretched way out of shape, often doubled in size, hemorrhaging internally and filled with coagulated liquid fats, pus, blood, gallstones, worms, cancer and just ungodly goop that was literally unidentifiable. Every student was shocked to see such advanced disease and degeneration in such young, supposedly healthy people.

WHAT I LEARNED IN MY CLINIC...
YOU ARE A VERY BUSY PERSON!

My clinic was in Hollywood and Malibu, California, and my patients were all from the entertainment industry. If you watch any movie that was filmed in the last 30 years, chances are your favorite scenes were filmed by a cameraman (who was on the program in this book), the audio people, the lighting staff or if not someone behind the scenes, then maybe the actor, actress or even the director was on my program. In spite of the glitz and glamour that surrounds the movie industry, directors, producers, actors and actresses, movie industry people usually work long 16-hour days under impossible deadlines and tremendous stress. And when they're not working, they are

rushing from one appointment to the next. So as my patients, they didn't need me to give them more work than was necessary to get the job done.

So, I needed to develop healing programs that were EFFECTIVE, but also EASY enough for my patients to do at work. Most people can't take a week off every season just to cleanse and still pay their bills, so I needed to design a week-long cleansing and detoxification program that a person could do without quitting their job and becoming a hermit.

So the bottom line is not only that this program is effective, but, more importantly, that all of my patients were successful in easily completing my **5-Day LIVER Detox.**

WHY DO A SEASONAL CLEANSING?

Your body is really no different than your car. Like any machine, if you want it to last and give you the maximum lifespan that it was designed for, and give you years and years of trouble-free service, then it needs routine maintenance.

If you want to get the most miles out of your vehicle, then you have to follow a routine preventative maintenance program, just like the one that comes inside the glove compartment of every new car. You know, change the oil and oil filter every 5,000 miles, rotate the tires, change the air filter every 10,000, a tune-up in 20 or 25,000 miles, radiator flush, check the battery and so on. Any mechanic will tell you that if you want your car to last for years and years, you need to take care of it.

WHAT IF YOU COULD ADD 10 YEARS TO YOUR LIFE...BY JUST DOING A SIMPLE CLEANSE A FEW DAYS A YEAR?

In fact, you will also notice that the manufacturer's new car warranty is void if you do not follow the manufacturer's suggested maintenance program. In fact, the warrantee will also be voided if you don't use approved parts, lubricants, oils, filters and so on. In other words, the automobile's manufacturer will not guarantee your vehicle if you don't take care of it.

Well, in my lifetime, I have never heard of God personally coming down and telling anyone that if they don't follow the manufacturer's program that the guarantee will be void. But nevertheless, "God's Laws of Nature" dictate that if you do not follow a routine maintenance program using the proper fuels and fluids, if you do not follow a routine preventative maintenance program, as sure as the wind, your vehicle will prematurely break down and you will die.

Your body, like any machine, uses fuel to run and as it runs it creates waste products. To have your machine run its best, it is important to use the absolute best fuels and to periodically cleanse your internal parts. This is very important even when you live in the best of environments, but we live far from the best environment. This is the problem...

Regardless of the fact that the Average American dies in 70 or 75 years, most medical universities today like Stanford and others agree that the human body, if properly nourished and maintained, should last about 125 years. They say that the only reason it doesn't, the reason it is shortened by 50 YEARS, is because of our lifestyle. The air we breathe, the fluids we drink, the food we eat and the life we live, KILLS YOU FIFTY YEARS EARLY!!!

Yeah, OK, I have been called "the toughest Natural Healing Doctor On The Block" and also the "Dirty Harry of Natural Healers." And I know that some of my Natural Healing Routines, my Incurables Program and some of my Clinical Herbal Formulations and Dosages can make even the most diehard health fanatics get weak in the knees and cry for mommy.

AND I KNOW THAT YOU'VE HEARD, "THIS GUY'S TOUGH" AND THAT MY PROGRAMS ARE EVEN TOUGHER.

I know some of my programs are tough, because I've done them all to heal myself. But when death is knocking at your door, and time has run out, it's time to put the pedal to the metal and pull out all of the stops. People need to understand. . .that while Natural Healers and Herbalists pussyfoot around with minimal dosages and scented candles, and play politically correct games with government agencies to get recognized. . . medical doctors are sharpening their scalpels and getting ready to cut your ass off, fry you with radiation and fill your body with the most concentrated poisons in their arsenal.

In my clinic, I learned that to literally save my patients from killer diseases I had to match the medical doctors level in intensity, but with Natural Healing Programs and Herbal Formulations and Dosages. So, I literally tried to kill my patients with water, juices, flushing and fasting, raw food, hydrotherapy, movement, herbal medicines and new positive emotional habits. I made them blow up and destroy their lives, the way they lived that caused their disease in the first place. This is how I helped literally thousands save their lives and HEAL THEMSELVES, after the medical doctors gave up and sent them home to rot and die.

BUT. . .THE PROGRAM IN THIS BOOK IS NOT TOUGH! IN FACT, IT'S VERY SIMPLE, EASY AND FAST!

Besides my life-saving programs, I also spent decades in my clinic developing and refining the most effective programs for SEASONAL CLEANSING AND DETOXIFICATION for my patients who were not dying, for my patients who had minor health problems or who were healthy and just wanted to stay that way.

Many of my patients, before they came to my clinic, had done these Overnight Miracle Flushes, 24-Hour Detox Programs or 2-Day Quick Cleanses you see in health food stores or hear about… and discovered for themselves that they didn't work or weren't thorough. What I know is that the average person needs about five days to get the old toxic accumulations out of their liver.

I also quickly learned that when my patients failed to stay on my cleansing program (they would say that they fell off, but it looked more like leaping off to me) their failure always took place on a weekend, not a weekday. Friends called for a last minute party, you forgot someone was having a get together, whatever, but trying to follow a detox routine on a weekend is a set up for failure.

Therefore, I discovered that a **5-Day Detox Program** done Monday through Friday was not only long enough to be completely effective but also, by being during the work week, it gave my patients the best chance at succeeding and completing the program.

MY 5-DAY LIVER DETOX IS:

▸ **Effective enough to FLUSH out your liver and REMOVE old toxic, poisonous waste.**

▸ **Powerful enough to FLUSH GALLSTONES, sludge and sediment from your gallbladder.**

▸ **PROTECTS and COATS your liver cells from future damage.**

▸ **And so EASY to do that you really won't notice the effort it takes, the five days will fly by.**

▸ **And in five days, you'll FEEL BETTER and have MORE ENERGY than you've had in years.**

Dr. Schulze's
5-Day LIVER Detox

Cleanse, detoxify and disinfect your liver and gallbladder

KIT INCLUDES: L-GB Formula, Detox Tea, Detox Formula, Fresh Breath Plus, Quick Start Directions, and Book: "Create Powerful Health Naturally, with Dr. Schulze's 5-Day Liver Detox"

▸ **Triple your energy and helps create Powerful Health**

▸ **PROTECTS and coats your liver cells and helps eliminate harmful, dangerous contaminants**

▸ **Flushes, dissolves and removes hardened sediment from the gallbladder**

▸ **Cleans your blood of unhealthy accumulated deposits**

...ALL IT TAKES IS 5 DAYS!

CHAPTER FIVE
DR. SCHULZE'S 5-DAY LIVER DETOX

I created my 5-Day Detox Program as an entry-level cleanse for all my patients. This program is an EASY cleanse that anyone can do.

After my patients started taking their **SuperFood Plus** on a regular basis and then did my **5-Day BOWEL Detox**, and their bowel was working normally, it was then time to do their first detoxification program. If you are ill, you can start my **5-Day LIVER Detox** IMMEDIATELY! You don't have to do my 5-Day BOWEL Detox first, just add the **Intestinal Formula #1** to the following program.

I give you my guarantee that you will feel physically better, more alive and more energetic after five days on this program. Also, you will feel better about yourself and your life too!

Come on friends, don't take this program (or life for that matter) too seriously. Just do it—jump right in! Next Monday sounds like a good time to start to me, and if it's already Tuesday, how about a 4-day cleanse? LOOK, any of you out there who think that this might be a little inconvenient or cramp your busy lifestyle, well, all I can tell you is that once people end up in the hospital, under the knife, they wish they would have done it 20 times. But more importantly, everyone should experience a few days of a juice flush and a few days on raw foods. For my patients, this program turned their health and their life around.

The Liver/Gallbladder Flush Drink and Herbal Formulae stimulate the liver to produce more bile and get the bile moving through the gallbladder and ducts. This action unblocks and unconstipates the liver and gallbladder and even dissolves and removes hardened sediments from gallbladder. **This is what will clean and detoxify your liver and gallbladder and what you need to START.**

My program is two days of a Purifying Raw Food Program and three days of a Juice Fast.

YES, I designed my **5-Day Detox Program** to be done during the week, at work or during your regular weekly routine. Look, nobody wants to do a cleanse or detox on the weekend. And usually, if you are silly enough to plan it that way, the phone rings, friends or relatives call, and the next thing you know, you've blown it. Weekend fun, friends, parties and eating are all a big part of this.

5-DAY DETOX DAILY ROUTINE: DO THESE 8 STEPS EVERY DAY

STEP 1: Upon arising drink 8 oz. of distilled or purified water.

STEP 2: Prepare and drink the **Liver/Gallbladder Flush Drink** (see How to Make Dr. Schulze's **Liver/Gallbladder Flush Drink** on page 52).

STEP 3: 15-20 minutes after drinking your **Liver/Gallbladder Flush Drink**, drink two cups of Detox Tea (see Dr. Schulze's **Detox Tea** directions on page 53). Put 2 droppersful of my **L-GB Formula** in each cup of tea (consume total of 4 droppersful) or have the tonic separately in one ounce of water.

STEP 4: Finally, take 3 droppersful of my **Detox Formula**. This formula is my strongest tasting, so you can put it in a little grape juice, if you wish.

STEP 5: One hour later, drink your **SuperFood Plus** Morning Nutritional Drink.

> **SuperFood Plus Directions:**
> In a blender, mix 8 ounces of organic fresh fruit juice, 8 ounces of pure water, 1/2 cup of fresh organic fruit and 2 tablespoons of **SuperFood Plus**.

STEP 6: Repeat the same dosage of the **Detox Tea** & **L-GB Formula** two more times during the day, consuming a total of 6 cups of **Detox Tea** and 12 droppersful of the **L-GB Formula** a day.

STEP 7: Repeat the same dosage of my **Detox Formula** four more times during the day, consuming a total of 3 droppersful five times a day.

STEP 8: Continue with the Food and Juice Program as outlined on the next page.

THE FOOD & JUICE PROGRAM

THIS PROGRAM IS 2 DAYS OF A PURIFYING RAW FOOD PROGRAM AND 3 DAYS OF A JUICE FLUSH.

Days 1 & 5 (Raw Food)

Breakfast: If you're hungry before lunchtime you may have fruit, diluted fruit juice and fruit smoothies. Stop all fruit and fruit juice at least one hour before lunch. While on this program, it is best not to mix fruits and vegetables.

Lunch: For lunch, you can have fresh raw vegetable juices, raw vegetables alone or in salads, sprouts, potassium broth (see directions on page 56) and herb teas. You may use dressings for your salads and vegetables if you like, using olive oil, avocado, raw apple cider vinegar, lemon juice, garlic, onions and any herbs and spices.

Afternoon snack: Raw vegetables, raw vegetable salads, diluted vegetable juices, sprouts, potassium broth and herb teas. All vegetable foods and juices must be stopped by 6 pm.

Dinner: Diluted fruit juices, fruit, fruit smoothies, fruit salads, water and herb teas.

Days 2, 3 & 4 (Juice Flush)

Now, we begin the 3-day fast. Consume at least one gallon (128 ounces) of liquid a day. That's eight 16-ounce servings a day. If you get hungry, drink more liquid!!!

Mornings: Start with water, your morning flush, herbal teas/tonics and your morning **SuperFood Plus** drink.

Mid-mornings: Diluted fruit juices, herb teas and water until noon.

Afternoons: Diluted vegetable juices, potassium broth, herb teas, and water until evening.

Evenings: Diluted fruit juice, herb teas and water in the evening.

Day 5 (Raw Food)

Day #5 is the day you will be breaking your fast. Your food program will be the same as Day #1. Breaking your fast is a very important part of this program. Chew your food slowly and mix each mouthful with plenty of saliva. Eat until you are satisfied, not full. You can always eat more, if you are still hungry. Chew everything to a liquid pulp.

HOW TO MAKE DR. SCHULZE'S 2-MINUTE LIVER/GALLBLADDER FLUSH DRINK

TOOLS

- Blender (any)
- 1 measuring cup (at least 16 oz.)
- 1 water glass (at least 20 oz.)
- 1 manual citrus juicer
- 1 knife (wider is better)
- 1 tablespoon

(FOR 1 FLUSH DRINK)

- 3-4 juice oranges, 1 lemon and 1 lime (enough for 8 oz.)
- 1-5 cloves of Organic Garlic
- 1 inch of fresh, Organic Ginger
- 1-5 tablespoons of Olive Oil (extra-virgin, cold-pressed organic)
- 8 oz. distilled or filtered Water

STEP 1: PUT 8 OZ. OF FRESH JUICE IN YOUR BLENDER

NOTE: During Spring or Summer, mix the juice of 1 lemon, 1 lime and enough oranges to make 8 oz. of a citrus combination juice. During Fall or Winter, mix 8 ounces of fresh apple or grape juice or an apple/grape combination juice.

STEP 2: ADD 1 TO 5 CLOVES OF GARLIC

(1 clove for DAY ONE, 2 for DAY TWO... until you reach 5 cloves by DAY FIVE)
NOTE: Do not chop the Garlic, just throw it in whole, the blender will do the rest. The best way to peel garlic is to smash it under the flat side of a knife, the peel will just slip off. Use medium sized cloves. (Use larger or smaller cloves, depending on your garlic tolerance.)

STEP 3: ADD 1 PIECE OF FRESH, ORGANIC GINGER ROOT (ABOUT 1 INCH LONG)

NOTE: Do not peel it. The blender will liquefy it.

STEP 4: FINALLY ADD:

- ▸ 8 oz. of distilled or filtered Water
- ▸ 1 to 5 tablespoons of Olive Oil (1 tablespoon for DAY ONE, 2 for DAY TWO...until you reach 5 tablespoons by DAY FIVE)

STEP 5: BLEND ALL OF THESE INGREDIENTS IN THE BLENDER FOR ABOUT 60 SECONDS AND DRINK!

STEP 6: DON'T FORGET! 15-20 MINUTES AFTER DRINKING YOUR LIVER/ GALLBLADDER FLUSH DRINK, PREPARE AND DRINK 2 CUPS OF DETOX TEA (SEE PG 63)

NOTE: Put 2 droppersful of my L-GB Formula in each cup of tea (total of 4 droppersful) or have the tonic separately in an ounce of water or an apple/grape combination juice.

Take this shopping list to the store, get these ingredients and you will be set up to do my entire **5-Day LIVER Detox Kit!**

▶ **15-20 Organic Juice Oranges**
It is important to use organic when you are flushing, because you don't want to put toxic, poisonous insecticides and pesticides into a drink that you are supposed to be cleaning your liver with.

▶ **5 Organic Lemons and 5 Organic Limes**

▶ **2 bulbs of Organic Garlic**
One bulb should do it, but why not have some extra garlic around?

▶ **5 inches of fresh, Organic Ginger Root**

▶ **3 gallons of distilled or purified Water**
This will make enough for your **Liver/Gallbladder Flush Drink**, as well as the 2 1/2 gallons you'll need for your **Detox Tea**.

▶ **24 oz. bottle of organic, extra-virgin cold-pressed Olive Oil**

REAL PEOPLE. REAL RESULTS.

"18 months ago my cholesterol was 1469, almost 1500, my triglycerides reached 8664, almost 9000! It was really scary. My head felt like the top of it could just explode, and my brain even felt like it was shaking, along with the rest of my body. I had to resort to nerve medication, and I tried the drugs to lower cholesterol, but found it was damaging my liver. I was hospitalized 3 times with pancreatitis, and I had another 4 attacks after, but just stayed home and survived. The hospital stays were complete nightmares. No one I have ever talked to, no doctor or lab worker, had ever heard of someone with cholesterol and triglyceride levels so HIGH and still be ALIVE.

I did the LIVER FLUSH 5 times in a row, as well as the whole Incurables Program. I passed two tumors with 'tentacles' and hundreds of small green stones. After a year on the programs, my cholesterol is now 158 and my triglycerides are down to 444! I thank God for the information arriving when it did! May God bless you and guide you in your adventure! If I could do it, I know you can do it too!! My prayers are with you. Love in Christ."

— *J.K., Mound City, MO*

"I was doubled over in pain, and the doctors wanted to get rid of my gallbladder. Instead, I did your Liver and Gall Bladder Program. The pain was gone immediately and in 5 days, I went back to the doctor and he said my gallstones were gone."

— *L.Q., Boca Raton, FL*

HOW TO MAKE DR. SCHULZE'S DETOX TEA

Put six rounded tablespoons of **Detox Tea** into 60 ounces of distilled water. Be sure to use only stainless steel or glass cookware. Let the tea sit in the water overnight. In the morning, heat up to a boil, reduce heat and let simmer for 15 minutes. Strain the herbs, do not discard them, let the tea cool a bit, but use it hot. This will give you enough tea for your six cups for the day. Put the used herbs back into the pot, add three tablespoons of fresh herbs and 60 ounces of distilled water. Let sit overnight and repeat whole process. Keep adding new herbs to old ones for three days, then discard all herbs and start over.

Detox Tea is cleansing and detoxifying to the entire digestive tract. Brew some today! **SUGGESTED DOSAGE: 2 cups, 3 times daily.**

Potassium Broth Recipe

This is a great tasting addition to your cleansing program. It will flush your system of toxins, acid and mucous, while giving you concentrated amounts of minerals.

▶ Fill a large pot with peelings of five potatoes, peelings of five carrots, five whole chopped beets, two chopped whole onions, five cloves of garlic, five stalks of whole chopped celery and the remaining dark beet greens.

▶ Add hot peppers to taste. Add enough distilled water to just cover vegetables and simmer on very low temperature for 1–4 hours. Strain and drink only the broth. Make enough for two days, and refrigerate the leftover broth. Use only organic vegetables! We do not want to consume any toxic, immune suppressive insecticides, pesticides or inorganic chemical fertilizers, while we are on a detoxification program.

My broth will flush you out and build you up. Start it now!

EMERGENCY
GALLBLADDER ATTACK TREATMENT

1 STOP EATING ALL FOOD immediately, which is a good idea with any acute illness. Take 4 droppersful of my Digestive Tonic and 4 droppersful of my L-GB Formula in an ounce of warm water, immediately.

2 PREPARE AND DRINK A LIVER/GALLBLADDER FLUSH DRINK. In an emergency, fresh apple-lemon juice is preferred, but any juice will work. Use at least 3 cloves of Garlic and 3 tablespoons of Olive Oil.

3 LIE ON YOUR RIGHT SIDE WITH A HOT PACK OVER YOUR LIVER. Castor Oil packs over the liver are very beneficial, as is hot and cold hydrotherapy.

4 15 MINUTES LATER DRINK 2 CUPS OF HOT, STRONG DETOX TEA with 6 droppersful of my L-GB Formula in each cup.

5 WHEN THE PAIN HAS SUBSIDED A BIT, GIVE YOURSELF A HIGH ENEMA. Relax, take an hour to do it.

6 For any spasmodic pain and cramping in the liver, TAKE AN ADDITIONAL 4 DROPPERSFUL OF MY DIGESTIVE TONIC AND 1/2 TO 1 DROPPERFUL OF LUNG TONIC in an ounce of water.

NOTE: If the pain persists after an hour, repeat all of these steps using 3 cloves of Garlic and 5 tablespoons of Olive Oil.

I don't recall any patient ever having to do this entire routine more than twice, before they got relief. The patient should then immediately start on my 5-Day LIVER Detox using the Liver and Gallbladder Flush Drink and my L-GB Formula, Detox Tea and Detox Formula. Remember, a gallbladder attack should be a wake-up call to change a person's lifestyle to a liver-friendly one.

A Letter From A More "Enlightened" Doctor About Dr. Schulze's 5-Day DETOX Program

Dear Dr. Schulze,

I have performed many cholecystectomies (surgical removal of the gallbladder) on my patients, during my professional career as a surgeon. In the past, I felt that your treatments, specifically your Liver and Gallbladder Flush, were quite harsh. But after reading about another doctor's positive experience with the Liver and Gallbladder Flush, I decided to try it myself and on my wife. Subsequently, I have had my patients do it also.

I am now convinced that the Flush is not only **safe**, but **effective** in cleansing the gallbladder, the liver and even the entire body, resulting in energy and stamina galore. Considering the degenerative change in people's present day lifestyle, **I now find that I am in agreement with what you recommend, particularly your 5-Day BOWEL Detox and your 5-Day LIVER Detox.**

Secondly, in the past I was often baffled by patients that would continue to have the same pain and complaints, after I removed their gallbladder. Particularly Post Cholecystectomy Biliary Dyskinesia (after surgical gallbladder removal the flow of bile is still interrupted). What we surgeons had never considered is that there may also be stones that could be lodged in the liver.

When surgeons do a cholecystectomy, they render only a partial treatment, with nary a thought that they might be leaving stones behind in the liver, thus sometimes causing a reoccurrence of the same problem after surgery.

Since today, surgical removal of liver stones is impossible, **why not recommend your non-invasive, painless liver flush to remove the stones both in the liver and the gallbladder?** And, give the patient a total cure! The Liver Flush is a simple procedure that any patient can do for themselves on the advice of the healthcare provider. Your Liver Cleanse requires no hospitalization, the necessary ingredients are inexpensive and readily available, the instructions are simple and the procedure is not uncomfortable nor distasteful.

Yours truly,
—T.H. M.D.,F.A.C.S.

what will create
Powerful Health"

Dr. Schulze's
ORIGINAL CLINICAL FORMULAE
Since 1979

HERBAL
FORMULAE
THAT WORK!
GUARANTEED!
Since 1979

5-DAY
Liver Detox

anse, detoxify and disinfect your liver and gallbladder

T INCLUDES: L-GB Formula, Detox Tea, Detox Formula, Fresh Breath Plus, Quick Start Directions,
and Book: "Create Powerful Health Naturally, with Dr. Schulze's 5-Day Liver Detox"

CHAPTER SIX
DR. SCHULZE DESCRIBES HIS HERBAL FORMULAE

Stimulate, cleanse and protect your liver and gallbladder and rid the body of parasites.

L-GB FORMULA

▶ **FLUSHES and DETOXIFIES the liver and gallbladder**

▶ **PROTECTS liver cells from damage and eliminates parasites**

▶ **CLEANS the gallbladder and removes hardened sediment**

▶ **A HEALTHY liver cleans your blood and prevents disease**

Botanical Ingredients:

Milk Thistle Seed, Dandelion Root, Oregon Grape Root, Gentian Root, Wormwood Leaf, Mojave Chaparral Herb, Black Walnut Hull, Hawaiian Yellow Ginger Root, Garlic Bulb, Fennel Seed, Artichoke Leaf

Your liver is your blood filter. Every second of every day, it filters, traps, neutralizes, kills and eliminates poisons that you inhale, ingest and absorb. From common poisonous chemicals in the home, workplace or even on your dinner plate, to prescription drug residues, air pollution and worn out blood cells, there are literally millions of toxic trash bits circulating all over your body that your liver has to defend you against. Almost ALL cancer today is directly linked to toxic chemical exposure. Your liver is your defensive barrier. But, when modern living attacks your liver with a constant chemical barrage, it can't do its job of protecting you.

REAL PEOPLE. REAL RESULTS.

"I was diagnosed with Hepatitis in '99, and now it's 2004. I never had a liver transplant. My skin is clearer than it's ever been. My health just keeps getting better and better. My eyesight is getting better. My prescription for my glasses has dropped two times in the last two years."

– B.S., Los Angeles, CA

The herbs in this formula are famous for their ability to stimulate, cleanse and protect the liver and gallbladder and rid the body of parasites. Milk Thistle contains many phytochemicals, three chief ones being silibinin, silydianin and silychristin. These three plant chemicals are often collectively referred to as silymarin. There are many ways in which these plant chemicals protect and heal your liver, too many for this book. But, two main ones are protection and regeneration. The phytochemicals in Milk Thistle actually strengthen the structure of the hepatocytes (liver cells) skin or membrane, which prevents the penetration of known liver toxins.

These protective chemicals also stimulate the action of the nucleolar polymerase A, resulting in an increase in ribosomal protein synthesis and thus stimulating the regeneration of damaged liver cells and stimulating the formation of new liver cells. These chemicals are so powerful they can even protect you from some of the most lethal poisons on the planet, like Deathcap Mushrooms. Simply put, ingesting Milk Thistle is like putting a protective coating around your current liver cells, while it also speeds up repair of damaged cells and building new strong cells.

Oregon Grape Rootbark, Gentian Root, Wormwood Leaves and Dandelion Root are some of the most bitter plants on the planet and are all classic bitter liver tonic herbs. They contain phytochemicals like berberine alkaloids and volatile oils, which stimulate the liver to produce more bile to flush out the bile ducts and gallbladder.

Black Walnut Hulls, Wormwood and Garlic are strong ANTI-PARASITICAL plants. Parasite infestation is a fact of life. One cubic inch of choice beef can have over 1,000 living parasite larvae waiting to hatch in your body. Over 65% of fresh fish tested had toxic levels of bacteria and parasites. Chicken is even worse. I've had hundreds of patients expel toilet bowls full of intestinal parasites, tape worms over 30 FEET LONG and also kill cellular parasites with this formula. It works best if used in conjunction with both Intestinal Formula #1 and #2. Use if parasites are suspected, or if there has been a history of bowel problems, constipation, eating of animal products, prolonged illness, disease and degeneration. If you have been exposed to any toxic substances, or drank alcohol or other harmful beverages, this formula is for you. It is also beneficial if you have had high cholesterol, blood fats or any family history of liver or gallbladder problems. Many believe that anyone who has cancer or any immune dysfunction had a weak, congested liver to begin with. Even if a person has had their gallbladder removed, these herbs will still be effective to clean the liver and bile ducts.

The **Detox Tea** has numerous health benefits. It is literally an all-purpose herbal tonic. It is a powerful stimulant, especially to the stomach, liver and digestive side of the pancreas. It also cleanses the skin and detoxifies the blood, liver and gallbladder and is the perfect tea to use after the **Liver Flush Drink.** It stimulates your liver to produce more bile and then flushes away the bile and fats that congest your liver and gallbladder.

This tea is an excellent coffee replacement. It tastes good and has no caffeine.

DETOX TEA

▶ **DETOXIFIES the blood, liver and gallbladder**

▶ **STIMULATES and cleanses the entire digestive tract**

▶ **ELIMINATES gas and indigestion**

▶ **INCREASES the flow of urine**

Botanical Ingredients:
Dandelion Root, Burdock Root, Cardamon Seed, Ginger Root, Pau d'Arco Bark, Cinnamon Bark, Clove Bud, Fennel Seed, Licorice Root, Juniper Berry, Black Peppercorn Uva Ursi Leaf, Horsetail Herb, Parsley Root, Orange Peel

Ginger Root, Cardamon Seed, Fennel Seed, Cinnamon Bark, Black Peppercorns and Clove Bud are famous classic digestive herbs. They are extremely effective and have been a part of traditional Chinese, Indian, European and American herbal medicine for centuries. They are specifics for dyspepsia (basically gas), cramps, colic, bloating, indigestion, heartburn and nausea. They contain essential oils, that stimulate ALL aspects of digestion, from saliva excretion and digestive juice stimulation to antispasmodic, and even stimulate the villi of the small intestine for better assimilation.

Cardamon Seeds, Roasted Dandelion Root, Burdock Root and Orange Peel all stimulate the liver to excrete more bile. While Cardamon has essential oils that cause this hepatic action, the three later herbs all contain bitter hepatic stimulating phytochemicals. Dandelion and Burdock also stimulate the kidneys to excrete more urine, along with the Horsetail Herb and Parsley Root. Juniper Berries and Uva Ursi Leaf are also diuretics and urinary tract disinfectants. They make you urinate more and destroy urinary infections. Pau d'Arco Inner Bark is a classic South American immune stimulant and Licorice Root is soothing and healing to the lining of the entire digestive tract.

Some of the botanicals in this politically incorrect herbal formula have been vigorously attacked by our federal government and medical groups during the past century, some within the past 10 years.

Some of these herbs have been illegal to use, like Chaparral, which was outlawed for almost 5 years. Suppliers stopped selling it and herbalists sucked up politically. Instead, I harvested my own in the California deserts and continued to use it. After all, in my clinic, potent healing ability dictated which herbs I put in my formulations and used with my patients, NOT politics. How could I look a patient in the eye who was suffering and tell them that I know what helps, but legally I can't sell it to you? Because I continued to use this herb during its prohibition, this became just one of the reasons my clinic was shut down. Other botanicals in the formula are highly discouraged by medical doctors like Lobelia Seed, Poke Root, even Red Clover Blossoms. Consequently, many herbalists (myself included), have been arrested and incarcerated for even discussing the benefits of these types of herbs, because of their association with treating cancer and chronic disease. Having said all of this, I must tell you that the herbs in this formula are classic and traditional blood and lymph cleansing tonics and the ones that I used successfully for many years in my clinic.

DETOX FORMULA

▸ **The most powerful DETOX formula available anywhere**

▸ **CLEANS accumulated toxins and poisons out of the body's blood and lymphatic system**

▸ **PROMOTES healthy skin and complexion**

Botanical Ingredients:

Red Clover Blossom, Mojave Chaparral Herb & Resin, Oregon Grape Root, Burdock Root, Yellow Dock Root, Poke Root, Goldenseal Root, Fresh Garlic Bulb, Lobelia Herb Seed, Habanero Pepper

This formula is based on the famous Hoxey Formula, Dr.

Christopher's Red Clover Combination (both herbalists were arrested on numerous occasions for these formulations) and many similar powerful alternative (blood cleansing) formula from around the world. These herbs are used in herbal medical clinics worldwide for scrubbing the accumulated toxins and poisons out of the body's blood, fat and cells and also heralded for their efficacy.

The following is common knowledge from highly respected and accepted medical text. According to pharmacology manuals, Chaparral contains nordihydroguaiaretic acid. According to the Merck Index, this acid from Chaparral is listed as an anti-oxidant with a Therapeutic Category, as an anti-neoplastic. According to Taber's Cyclopedic Medical Dictionary, an anti-neoplastic is "an agent that prevents the development, growth and proliferation of malignant cells (tumors)."

This is by far one of my most powerful and strong tasting herbal tonics. You will want to add your 3 droppersful to 1 ounce of strong apple or grape juice and knock it back. This is an herbal Jack Daniels, not a fine wine. Don't savor it. GET IT DOWN. You might even want a chaser.

CHAPTER SEVEN
FREQUENTLY ASKED QUESTIONS

The following are the most commonly asked questions and concerns about LIVER cleansing.

HOW MANY TIMES A YEAR SHOULD I DO THE CLEANSE, AND HOW LONG SHOULD I STAY ON THE FORMULAS WHEN I'M CLEANSING?

For the average person who's healthy and does not have any disease or illness, the great prevention is to have a one-week cleanse four times a year. That's a week during the Spring, Summer, Fall and Winter. Pick a week when you can, for five, six or seven days in a row, perform a cleanse, an oil change, a prevention. Clean yourself up. My patients who did that rarely ever had any health problems or ever got sick. And, the length of it is a week long. That's usually good enough for the person who

lives a good, healthy lifestyle to prevent any problems from happening. Now, if you're ill, certainly you can do it more often. And certainly if you're ill right now, you can extend it. Remember, my Incurables Program starts with a minimum of 30 days of juice fasting and health programs. So, you can cleanse for as long as you want. But the minimum is one week, four times a year.

DO I NEED TO RESERVE SPECIAL DAYS FOR DOING MY CLEANSE?

Everything in life works better when you prepare yourself for it. Mark out the days on your calendar at least a couple weeks in advance. It doesn't do you any good to wake up in the morning and say, "Hey, I'm going to do my cleansing routine," but you binged the weekend before and you open your refrigerator and there's nothing you need to start your cleansing routine. Just like anything else you want to succeed in, a little preparation will really help you in being successful.

IS JUICE FASTING MANDATORY?

Personally, if you want to get well, juice fasting is mandatory. My **5-Day Detox** is two days of raw foods and three days of juice fasting. If you do it Monday through Friday, Monday and Friday are raw foods and Tuesday, Wednesday, and Thursday are juice-fasting. When you go back into the last century, you look at any of the great natural healers and you'll see that juice fasting was a foundation of the programs they used to get well. I don't care who you study and who you look at. All my great teachers, like Paavo Airola and Dr. Bernard Jensen and Dr. John Christopher, used juice fasting as one of their primary healing tools. We should really call it juice flushing, because what you are doing is introducing a gallon a day or more of herb teas, distilled water, and fresh juices through your body that not only give you super nutrition but also flush out unwanted acids and salts and old minerals and toxic accumulations and chemicals. This is probably the greatest part

of a Natural Healing cleansing and detoxification routine. So do not skip your juice fasting. I have seen it create miracle after miracle in the clinic. Juice fasting is what you want to be doing.

However, having said that, you do not have to do the whole program. You know, some mornings I wake up (don't hesitate to try this) and I feel like I could use a **Liver Flush**, I feel a little sluggish. Or I feel like I could use a **Kidney/Bladder Flush**. So I make a **Liver Flush Drink** or a **Kidney Flush Drink** and I have it in the morning. And then, I just go about the rest of my day. Maybe have a **SuperFood Plus** drink a few hours later, and then a few hours after that I might have some lunch and then some dinner. So the point is, never hesitate to just wake up in the morning and do a flush drink, whether it's the **Liver/Gallbladder** or the **Kidney/Bladder.** You don't have to do the whole program.

I would rather see you modify the program all the way down to doing one flush drink, than not doing anything at all. Now, certainly it's optimum to add in the juice fasting. Some people ask this question because they have diabetes and they're afraid to do juice fasting. Let me tell you, I have had so many diabetics, both type one and type two, do my juice fasting and juice flushing programs. You have nothing to worry about. Just use your good smarts and your common sense, and you can do it, too. Because the program is much more powerful, both the **Liver/Gallbladder** and the **Kidney/Bladder**, if you do it with the whole **5-Day Detox**, which includes my 5-DAY Food Program.

CAN YOU MODIFY THE 5-DAY LIVER DETOX?

Well, I never really expected anybody to methodically follow exactly what I said to do. You would have to be a robot to be doing things that way. All I want you to do is your best. Of course, the times can be modified. They can be modified to your lifestyle, and they can be modified to your workplace, because you're probably doing the cleanse at your workplace. What I would like you to think about is this: at the end of the day, I would like you to have consumed all the foods, all the juices and all the herbs and herbal formulas that I suggested. And, space them out as much as possible. Do you have to follow my program down to the minute or the hour? No, you

don't. And you'd probably have a very hard time trying. In fact, any patient that follows any of those programs to a tee, well, I would worry about them. They may be a little bit neurotic. Sure, modify it to where it works with your life. The bottom line is I want you to do it. You're never going to get well if you look at my **5-Day Detox** and study it, but figure you can't ever do it perfectly so you won't do it at all. Do your best. That's all I'm asking of any of you is, do your best at doing the program.

DO YOU SUGGEST DOING THE DETOX FORMULA ALONG WITH THE 5-DAY LIVER DETOX?

In the clinic, whenever I had a patient do my five-day cleansing and detoxification program, they did one of two things on top of it. They either consumed one entire two-ounce bottle of my **Detox Formula**, or they consumed one entire two-ounce bottle of the **Echinacea Plus**. The idea is, when you're doing that cleanse and detoxification program, you either want to be scrubbing out your blood even more with the great herbal blood cleansers or boosting your immune system. So if you do the blood cleansers in the Spring, then boost your immune system in the Summer. But definitely do the **Detox Formula**, or **Echinacea Plus**, during your five-day cleanse. And remember to consume one entire two-ounce bottle.

WHAT ARE THE BENEFITS OF TAKING INTESTINAL FORMULA #1 AND #2, WHILE DOING THE 5-DAY LIVER DETOX?

The bottom line is that when you flush your liver and gallbladder out, the waste that you flush out goes directly into your intestines and colon. If your bowel is not working properly or you are constipated this toxic waste cannot get out of your body.

Remember, your bowel is your major elimination organ for your solids. Some of the herbs in the **Intestinal Formula #1** also stimulate your liver and gallbladder, so this helps with their cleansing. Also, by keeping your bowel clean, this takes the pressure off your kidneys and bladder and certainly will assist in their cleaning. So, it is very important to use your **Intestinal Formula #1** and your **Intestinal Formula #2.** In other words, do your **5-Day BOWEL Detox** during my **5-Day Detox,** whether you're doing the **Liver/Gallbladder Flush** or the **Kidney/Bladder Flush.**

HOW DO I IMPROVE MY DIGESTION AFTER I'VE DONE YOUR 5-DAY LIVER DETOX?

First of all, continue on **Intestinal Formula #1**. That speeds up your elimination, which will help take the pressure, especially any back pressure, off of your whole digestive tract. So don't forget to use your **Intestinal Formula #1**. Secondly, use my **Digestive Tonic**. It is a godsend for people with all types of cramps and colic and indigestion and heartburn. Two droppersful in an ounce of water, knock it back, and your digestive problems are gone. It's one of my personal favorites. And, lastly, there's my **Detox Tea**, and it's a wonderful digestive tea. There are so many herbs in it to aid your digestion, so if you're a tea drinker this is a good formula for you, and it will help your digestion out, too.

CAN I REALLY FLUSH THE STONES OUT OF MY GALLBLADDER AND AVOID HAVING IT REMOVED?

Absolutely, you can. I've had thousands of patients whose

gallbladders were ultra-sounded, x-rayed, packed full of rocks and they got rid of their rock collection using this program. Gallbladder surgery is the most ridiculous surgery. It's so stupid to cut a weak or sick organ out of the body. It's like cutting your bowel out, because it's constipated. And I shouldn't laugh, because many colostomies were performed on my constipated patients, before I got my hands on them. Surgery is only for people who won't change their lives. In fact, almost all of medicine is for people who won't change their lives and take responsibility for themselves. So, I can assure you that the **5-Day LIVER Detox** will do exactly that. It will flush any stones, pebbles, or rocks out of your gallbladder, through your digestive tract and you'll eliminate them. In fact, I'm holding in my hand right here a letter from a surgeon, a medical doctor, who performed many cholecysectomies (surgical removals of gallbladders). Now with his patients, he does my **5-Day LIVER Detox** and finds it to work in every instance, and doesn't do the surgery anymore. That is a very new type of medical doctor! Now we can give him some applause for seeing the light. I can assure you that the **5-Day LIVER Detox** will do the job.

WHICH 5-DAY DETOX SHOULD I DO FIRST, THE LIVER/GALLBLADDER CLEANSE OR THE KIDNEY/BLADDER?

There's a couple ways to make this decision. The first has to do with your history. Have you had any problems with your liver and gallbladder? Have you had any gallbladder congestion? Do you have high cholesterol? Any history of hepatitis, or any family history of any liver or gallbladder problems? If you fall in that category, then yes, go ahead and start my **5-Day LIVER Detox**. On the other hand, if you've had kidney stones, kidney or bladder infections, frequent urination, or any family or personal history of kidney or bladder problems, then you should start with the **5-Day KIDNEY Detox**. If you haven't had any problems at all and have no family history of problems with either the liver, gallbladder, the kidney or bladder, then there's a very simple way to decide. If your eyes are light brown or brown, then I would suggest that you do the **5-Day LIVER Detox** for the first cleanse. And if you have blue eyes, then you should start with the **5-Day KIDNEY Detox.** And if you have green eyes, well, you can go either way. And then on your next seasonal cleanse, do the other program. Now, if you have problems with just one, you can do that flush for the first two or three seasonal cleanses, but at least once a year try the other flush and the other herbs. So if you do the **5-Day LIVER Detox** for Spring, Summer and Fall cleanses, then in the Winter do a **5-Day KIDNEY Detox**. You should at least do the other cleanse one time a year.

WILL I GET BETTER RESULTS DOING A LIVER PURGE, LIKE THE ONES THAT USE EPSOM SALTS AND OLIVE OIL?

There are many extreme programs out there, where you consume copious amounts of oil, copious amounts of citrus juice, Epsom salts, Coca-Cola… believe me, there are many of them out there. And only in maybe 1% of my patients' extreme cases would I find those necessary (but never the Coca-Cola). Generally, I would just repeat my **5-Day LIVER Detox** and **Liver Flush Drink**, and that would do the job. So I just want to caution people—there are a lot of extreme gallbladder flushes (or what people might call liver flushes), but that's not what we're talking about here. We're talking about five days of a vegan raw food program, and

within those five days, two to three days of juice fasting, along with my **Liver Flush Drink** and **Detox Tea** and **L-GB Formula**. People who do this program are shocked at how simple, easy, and effective my **Liver Flush Drink** and **5-Day LIVER Detox** can be.

HAVE YOU HEARD THE STUDIES LINKING TYLENOL WITH LIVER CANCER?

No, I haven't heard about the studies with Tylenol, but let me tell you something. All drugs have to be cleaned out of your blood by your liver, and all drugs kill your liver cells, therefore all drugs kill your liver. The more drugs you've taken, the more your liver is dead. Immediately start on my **L-GB Formula** that contains Milk Thistle, which is a liver cell protectant, so you protect whatever cells you have left, and then immediately think about doing my **5-Day LIVER Detox**, along with the **Liver Flush Drink**.

WHAT DO YOU THINK ABOUT CHELATION TREATMENTS?

I don't like them. Chelation is usually taking the blood out of your body and washing it, or adding something to the blood of your body to clean it up. Sometimes minerals, sometimes other things. Let me tell you something. This stuff called skin that covers our body should not be broken for any reason. I do not believe in any therapy that involves shots, needles or puncturing the skin.

WHAT IF I'M DIABETIC, OR IF I DON'T HAVE A GALLBLADDER, OR IF I HAVE HEPATITIS B? CAN I STILL DO THE CLEANSE?

The answer is yes, yes, yes, across the board. Don't use any of these excuses for not getting well. Because believe me, while you're futzing around with should I or shouldn't I cleanse, the doctors are grinding and sharpening their scalpels, they're fixing up their deadly chemotherapy and they're tuning in their laser and radiation beams. They're not going to fool around. You walk in a hospital, they're going to hit you hard and fast and you're not going to know what blasted you. So, don't let all of your piddly little problems and questions get in the way of you creating a new, healthy lifestyle and a great healing program to make yourself well.

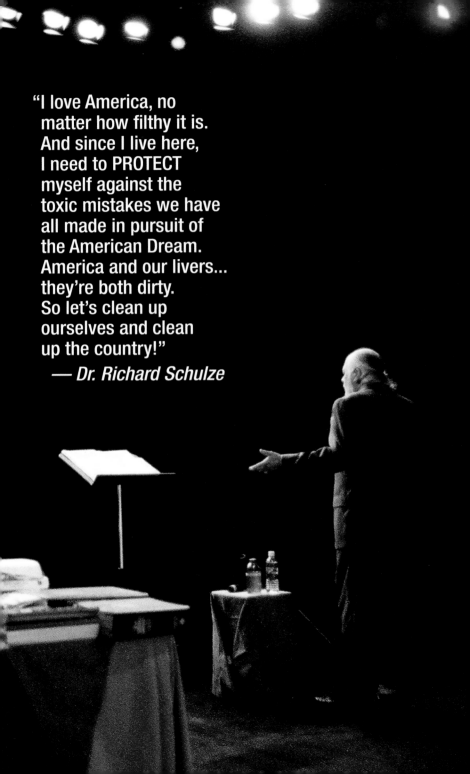

"I love America, no matter how filthy it is. And since I live here, I need to PROTECT myself against the toxic mistakes we have all made in pursuit of the American Dream. America and our livers... they're both dirty. So let's clean up ourselves and clean up the country!"

— *Dr. Richard Schulze*

CHAPTER EIGHT
FINAL THOUGHTS

My friend and CPA, Kirt, always says, "Look at the donut, not the hole." So let me be clear...I love America, even if it's filthy. I love my life and I LOVE LIVING IN AMERICA.

I learned long ago, that the best way to change anything is to start at home, not in the Senate, House of Representatives or in Washington, DC. So I take personal responsibility for the filthy state of our American water, earth and air, and I work to clean it up every day. You can help in an enormous way just by making better choices. I call it voting with your dollars. Choose to buy products from companies that are making an effort to not only stop polluting, but to also help clean up America.

If you want to know who the worst polluters are in your neighborhood, log on to www.scorecard.org sponsored by the Environmental Defense Fund. You just plug in your zip code and they will tell you who the bad guys are in your neighborhood. You can make a big difference just by not supporting these companies or, if you like their products, letting them know how you feel.

At my company, American Botanical Pharmacy, we are a National Leader in many areas of recycling and other earth friendly policies. We are one of the largest buyers of what we call really recycled paper in America. We not only promote the use of hemp instead of trees, but also use post-consumer recycled paper (which I call really recycled since pre-consumer recycled isn't recycled at all, it's just new paper that was not used and then resold). There, now I let that cat out of the bag. We also choose paper that comes from the cleanest paper mills that DON'T use chlorine to bleach the paper, which ends up in the nearby streams poisoning and killing fish, birds and other wildlife, including your wild children.

At American Botanical Pharmacy, we only use starch eco-foam packing peanuts instead of plastic foam. And if we do use plastic bubble wrap, it is 100% recycled. We shred all of our recycled office paper and then reuse it as shipping material. Almost all of our waste is recycled and we throw very little away.

We use organic herbs and foods not only because they are more potent, but also because they are not toxic. Every year in America, billions and billions of tons of poisonous chemicals are dumped and sprayed on our soil, to the point where most of American land is now poison.

Today, organic herbs are very popular and most herb companies are being forced to convert to using them, unfortunately not because they want to but because customers like you are demanding organic. But, unfortunately being grown organic and remaining organic and chemical-free until you put them in your mouth are two very different things. As far as I am aware and have been told by my many organic

farmers and suppliers, American Botanical Pharmacy is one of the ONLY COMPANIES in America that demands that the organic herbs we purchase are NOT GASSED with toxic ETHYLENE OXIDE, an industrial anti-bacterial gas that is proven to cause cancer and birth defects. Apparently, other herb companies simply cave in and go with the toxic crowd. You will never see this on their labels, but it is the industry standard. This gas after use is vented into the open air and one such herb supplier—in fact one of the biggest herb suppliers in America, one that supplies a large portion of herbal product manufacturers, Botanicals International in Southern California—was fined for polluting the air and endangering the nearby residents by letting ethylene oxide out of their herbal gas chambers.

Every day, you cast a big vote when you spend your money. You literally promote and support and build companies and corporations and put other ones out of business. You can make some companies that share your philosophy grow big and other ones disappear.

This is what is so great about the American economic system of supply and demand, unlike the old Communistic system of government controlled businesses where the people end up getting whatever big brother thinks you should have. In America when you buy any product, you promote that company, and when you don't buy the competitor's product, well, they are just one more step towards closing their doors and going out of business. If you think that your opinion or your choices don't matter, you are very wrong.

Make good informed choices with your purchases, not just the green-looking companies that give the green appearance, but really aren't doing the work. The commonplace nowadays is that most manufacturers stamp on their products that their product is recyclable (not recycled). What they should really say is that they have done nothing and we want you to do all of the work. Please support companies that make the health of our land, air and water as big a priority as making a good product. If you will help me do this, we can clean up America in a heartbeat and make it a safer and healthier place to live, grow up, work and play in.

Dr. Richard Schulze

DR. SCHULZE'S
HERBAL PRODUCT CATALOG

Dr. Schulze's
Catalog Includes...

▸ **Easy to understand descriptions of ALL his powerfully effective Herbal Formulae**

▸ **His common sense Natural Healing Wisdom and Clinical Experiences**

▸ **NEW Herbal Formulae and Clinical Detox Programs**

▸ **Plus many new inspiring Customer Testimonials and Healing Miracles**

CHAPTER EIGHT
ADDITIONAL RESOURCES

Get Well: How To Create Powerful Health

▶ Let Dr. Schulze introduce
you to his philosophies of
Natural Healing

▶ Learn the importance of
attitude, emotions and
spirituality in the quest for
health

▶ Listen to stories from
Dr. Schulze's clinic

▶ Learn Dr. Schulze's 20
simple and easy steps
toward a healthy new life

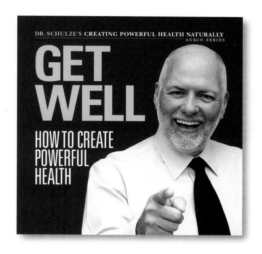

Ask for your FREE copy today!
Call 1-800-HERB-DOC (437-2362)
or visit us at WWW.HERBDOC.COM